THE PRACTICAL STRATEGIES SERIES
IN GIFTED EDUCATION

series editors
FRANCES A. KARNES & KRISTEN R. STEPHENS

Successful Strategies for Twice-Exceptional Students

Kevin D. Besnoy, Ph.D.

PRUFROCK PRESS, INC.

Printed in the United States of America.

ISBN-13: 978-1-59363-194-9
ISBN-10: 1-59363-194-4

At the time of this book's publication, all facts and figures cited are the most current available. All telephone numbers, addresses, and Web site URLs are accurate and active. All publications, organizations, Web sites, and other resources exist as described in the book, and all have been verified. The authors and Prufrock Press, Inc., make no warranty or guarantee concerning the information and materials given out by organizations or content found at Web sites, and we are not responsible for any changes that occur after this book's publication. If you find an error, please contact Prufrock Press, Inc. We strongly recommend to parents, teachers, and other adults that you monitor children's use of the Internet.

Prufrock Press, Inc.
P.O. Box 8813
Waco, Texas 76714-8813
(800) 998-2208
Fax (800) 240-0333
http://www.prufrock.com

Contents

The Practical Strategies Series in Gifted Education offers teachers, counselors, administrators, parents, and other interested parties up-to-date instructional techniques and information on a variety of issues pertinent to the field of gifted education. Each guide addresses a focused topic and is written by scholars with authority on the issue. Several guides have been published. Among the titles are:

- *Acceleration Strategies for Teaching Gifted Learners*
- *Curriculum Compacting: An Easy Start to Differentiating for High-Potential Students*
- *Enrichment Opportunities for Gifted Learners*
- *Independent Study for Gifted Learners*
- *Motivating Gifted Students*
- *Questioning Strategies for Teaching the Gifted*
- *Social & Emotional Teaching Strategies*
- *Using Media & Technology With Gifted Learners*

For a current listing of available guides within the series, please contact Prufrock Press at (800) 998-2208 or visit http://www.prufrock.com.

Introduction

As a young child, Frank W. Woolworth struggled in school. He had a difficult time keeping up with his classmates, and his teachers labeled him as "slow." Although he was not very successful in school, young Frank experienced a lot of success in the business world. In order to help his family, he began working in a local grocery store where he helped market products. His idea was to place 5-cent items near the checkout counter. Although this may not seem like an innovative idea today, it was revolutionary at the time. Frank Woolworth did not allow his "slow" label to prevent him from becoming a successful businessman. In 1879, he opened his first store in Utica, NY. By 1911, the F. W. Woolworth Company had more than 1,000 stores across the United States and in other countries. The success of F. W. Woolworth demonstrates that gifted students with learning disabilities can be successful. Yet, if twice-exceptional students are to maximize their potential, they need appropriate instructional strategies that enable them to utilize their strengths to compensate for their disabilities.

Although it is difficult to comprehend, it is possible for a child to be both gifted and learning disabled. Everyone with a vested interest in the well-being of gifted and learning disabled students must be committed to providing them with an appropriate education. To meet this goal, we must first understand how the gift and disability manifest themselves.

In order to provide proper instructional strategies for gifted students with learning disabilities, it is necessary to understand their learning and social-emotional characteristics. In order for twice-exceptional children to maximize their potential, teachers, parents, and students must work together. Intervention strategies must boost self-efficacy, promote areas of strength, and provide coping strategies to compensate for disabilities.

Hannah and Shore (1995) assert that gifted students with learning disabilities are stereotyped. Their giftedness implies that they have metacognitive prowess, yet their learning disability suggests they lack strong metacognitive skills. These opposing stereotypes make it difficult to adequately define the characteristics of twice-exceptional students. Susan Baum (1990) groups twice-exceptional students into one of three categories: those who have been identified as gifted, but whose learning disability is not recognized; those who have an identified learning disability, but whose giftedness is unknown; and those whose giftedness and learning disability go unnoticed, thus they appear to be average students.

Identified Gifted

Gifted students with slight learning disabilities tend to be easily identified. Baum (1990) acknowledges that this group scores high on achievement and IQ tests, allowing educators to readily identify them as gifted. However, this group has a propensity to be underachievers and, as they progress through school, this underachievement intensifies. Baum suggests that such underachievement can be attributed to poor self-concept or lack of motivation. Moreover, Vaidya (1993) indicates that students with learning disabilities find learning a difficult and painful process. As these students matriculate through school, they become more frustrated with the learning process, thus the disparity between potential and achievement widens. These students tend to have poor handwriting and spelling skills (Fetzer, 2000); have high verbal abilities (Little, 2001); and are forgetful, sloppy, and disorganized (Baum). Often, teachers and parents, knowing the potential these students have, become frustrated with the students' progress. According to Baum, concerned adults often believe these students only need to try harder in order to meet their potential. However, without appropriate intervention programs, increased effort is still not enough to generate achievement.

Brody and Mills (1997) note that these students' learning disabilities may go unrecognized for the majority of their education. This oversight is a real concern for these students because they do not have the necessary skills to capitalize on their talent. According to Baum (1990), although increased effort may be required for achievement, the real issue is how these students compensate for their disability. By identifying the disability, educators can teach twice-exceptional students appropriate social and educational coping skills.

Identified Learning Disabled

The second group of twice-exceptional students is the identified learning-disabled students whose giftedness remains unrecognized. Fetzer (2000) reports that these students are frequently placed in classes for students with learning disabilities. Generally speaking, they are usually well-behaved. Interestingly, their disabilities tend to depress their intellectual performance, and they are rarely referred for gifted services (Brody & Mills, 1997). The services these students receive merely address their disability. Baum (1990) states that parents and teachers become focused on the problem because they do not recognize the student's gifts. While these children often have high-level interests at home, little consideration is paid to their strengths and interests in school.

Furthermore, the learning disabled label places these students at risk for either not completing high school or completing school without the necessary knowledge, skills, and attitude to function successfully in adult life. In describing this population of twice-exceptional students, Baum (1990) explains that they begin to generalize their feelings of academic failure to an overall sense of inadequacy. Without appropriate interventions, these students struggle academically.

Unidentified Gifted or Learning Disabled

The third group of twice-exceptional students is children whose gifts and disabilities are both cloaked by average achievement. Brody and Mills (1997) assert that this is perhaps the largest group of twice-exceptional students. In reality, their gifts mask the disability and the disability masks their gifts (Baum, 1990). Although these students might excel in a specific subject, such as social studies, they tend to perform at grade level on achievement tests and in course work. In addition to their grade level work, these students tend to display appropriate classroom behavior. These two factors make it difficult to identify this population as twice-exceptional. Although the masked talents and disabilities might surface in specific content areas or be brought out by a teacher's unique teaching methods, Baum states that the disability is generally not discovered until college or adulthood.

Regardless of the category, all twice-exceptional students have distinguishing characteristics that must be addressed by teachers, parents, and school administrators. To meet their various needs, educators and parents must work together to improve intervention strategies (Baum, 1990; Brody & Mills, 1997; Winebrenner, 2003). Moreover, in order to be successful, gifted students with learning disabilities must receive instruction that attends to both their gifts and disability.

When helping twice-exceptional students it is important to be familiar with the laws regarding education and disabilities. Understanding the responsibilities of parents, teachers, school administrators, and the student, will prepare one to serve as an effective advocate. For many people outside the field of education (and many within) Section 504 of the Rehabilitation Act of 1973 and the Individuals with Disabilities Education Act (IDEA) are synonymous. However, these are actually two separate laws that have different ramifications for schools, parents, teachers, and students.

There are a few important similarities that warrant discussion. First, both laws are designed to protect individuals with disabilities. Next, each was created to ensure that individuals with disabilities are afforded the right to a free and appropriate public education. Finally, both laws require that protected individuals receive an individualized education.

While a few similarities exist, it is important for advocates to understand how each law affects gifted students with disabilities. Section 504 is a civil rights law that prohibits discrimination on the basis of disability in programs (both public and private) that receive federal funding. However, Section 504 does not guarantee an individualized education program. Rather, deBettencourt (2002) states that this law only requires school districts to make necessary accommodations, within reason, for students with disabilities.

Conversely, IDEA is an education act that provides federal funding to state and local education agencies in order to guarantee special education and related services to eligible students. The purpose of this law is to make certain that state and local education agencies provide students with disabilities a free and appropriate public education in the least restrictive environment.

According to Rosenfeld (n.d.), the purpose of Section 504 is to make society more accessible to students with disabilities. IDEA requires that schools offer remediation services in addition to the general programs available for students without disabilities (see Appendix A). The following sections present an overview of these rights with practical tips for developing appropriate Section 504 plans and Individualized Education Plans (IEPs).

Section 504

Disabilities, according to Section 504, are broadly defined. Under this law, individuals with a disability are those who have, have a history of having, or are perceived as having a physical or mental impairment that limits one or more life activities. In the education arena, learning is the major life activity that is limited as a result of the disability (Rehabilitation Act of 1973; Sevier County Department of Education, 2004a). The history or perception of having a disability only qualifies the individual for Section 504 protections if discrimination has taken place as a result of that history or perception (Yell, 1998). Examples of disabilities under Section 504, which may not be covered by IDEA, include physical injuries and/or other physical impairments, alcohol or drug addiction, and communicable diseases, including the HIV virus.

Students who are not covered by IDEA, but who are covered under Section 504, are entitled to receive a 504 Plan. The purpose of this plan is to detail the accommodations that need to be made to school buildings, classrooms, programs, or services to ensure that the student is provided equal access (see Appendix B). Modifications include, but are not limited to:

- redesign of equipment,
- reassignment of classes or other services to accessible sites,
- assignment of aides,
- alteration of existing facilities,
- new construction, and
- administration of medication (Sevier County Department of Education, 2004a; Smith, 2002).

Furthermore, each school program and activity must be readily accessible to persons with disabilities. Programs and services include, but are not limited to:

- counseling,
- competitive or recreational athletics,
- transportation,
- health services,
- special interest groups or clubs, and
- student employment (Sevier County Department of Education, 2004a; Smith, 2002).

Section 504—School and school district responsibilities

Schools and school districts must adhere to certain requirements in order to be in compliance with Section 504. Although special education personnel should be involved in guaranteeing that an individual school is in compliance with the law, the responsibility to manage the accommodations is left up to the school's general education program. In addition, student services provided by Section 504 are not to be paid for out of special education budgets. Specific school responsibilities include:

- appoint a Section 504 coordinator who is responsible for assisting schools in providing the necessary resources so that the various requirements of the law can be met;
- develop formal procedures by which grievances can be resolved;

- make certain that all district personnel are following Section 504 mandates;
- conduct continuous staff development regarding the meaning and requirements of the law; and
- identify and evaluate students who may qualify for services under Section 504, and provide a free and appropriate education for those who do qualify (Rehabilitation Act of 1973; Sevier County Department of Education, 2004a; Smith, 2002).

Section 504—Parent/guardian responsibilities

Parents and guardians can be effective advocates for their child. Just as schools have specific responsibilities, parents and guardians must also take responsibility by:

- communicating concerns with school officials early before problems escalate,
- becoming actively involved during Section 504 meetings, and
- providing support at home (Rehabilitation Act of 1973; Sevier County Department of Education, 2004a; Smith, 2002).

Section 504—Student responsibilities

Including the student in Section 504 meetings is important because it empowers students and gives them a feeling of control. It also provides them with an opportunity to express their educational needs. Finally, it enables students to see that school personnel are working to help these students succeed. Students' responsibilities include, but are not limited to:

- actively participating in the Section 504 meetings;
- cooperating with parents, teachers, and other school personnel; and
- familiarizing themselves with their rights in post-secondary programs (Sevier County Department of Education, 2004a; Smith, 2002).

Developing appropriate Section 504 plans can be a lengthy process. Making sure that physical, behavioral, and instructional accommodations are all met is difficult. If parents, teachers, and the student establish trusting relationships, an appropriate plan can be created.

Scenario:

Bill: A gifted student with a learning disability

> As a second grader, Bill was identified as gifted with an IQ over 140. However, he struggled with reading and his academic achievement was not commensurate with his ability. Concerned that Bill might have a learning disability, which can adversely affect a major life activity, his teacher referred him to the school's teacher support team. After reviewing his academic profile, the team contacted Bill's parents and decided to test Bill for a learning disability.
>
> The results of the test revealed that Bill had a reading disability, thus the team (including Bill's parents and Bill) designed a 504 plan. The accommodations included support in the use of advanced organizers and training in organizational strategies. The team determined that these strategies would be implemented in all educational settings, including the gifted education classroom. In addition, Bill's parents agreed to reinforce them at home.
>
> After an 8-week period, Bill's academic performance improved. Although he was not yet performing at his ability level, he was achieving better than average, thus the discrepancy was not significant enough for IDEA eligibility. The team decided to continue Bill's accommodations and to review his progress in 3 years.

IDEA

In the fall of 2004, the Congress reauthorized the IDEA legislation. The reauthorized act recognizes gifted students with disabilities. As a result, the U.S. Department of Education now recognizes twice-exceptional children as one of the groups that can be considered for educational grants (IDEA, 2004; NAGC, 2004). By recognizing the needs of gifted students with disabilities, the legislation permits funds to be granted to organizations interested in conducting research regarding twice-exceptional students.

Disability categories under the IDEA include:

- Autism,
- mental retardation,
- deaf-blindness,
- hearing impairments (including deafness),
- speech or language impairments,
- visual impairments (including blindness),
- multiple disabilities (excluding deaf-blindness),
- serious emotional disturbance,
- orthopedic impairments,
- traumatic brain injury,
- other health impairments, and
- specific learning disabilities.

Many children have disabilities, yet this does not qualify them automatically for special education services. In order to receive special education services under IDEA, the disability must have an adverse effect on educational performance. Federal law requires that the child should be evaluated in all areas related to the suspected disability. He or she should also be tested in any other areas that relate to the suspected disability, including health, social and emotional status, and motor abilities. Notice must be given to parents before a child is evaluated for the first time, and parental approval is required prior to conducting the evaluation. After the presence of a disability that adversely affects academic performance has been determined, a team is assembled to create an IEP.

An IEP is a plan that includes information regarding the child's strengths, weaknesses, and needs; a statement of measurable annual goals; and an explanation of modifications and activities in which the child will or will not participate. Once children enter high school, a transition plan is created that details how the child will move from high school to post-secondary education and careers.

The IEP team ideally consists of the student, parents, regular education teachers, special education teachers, gifted education teachers, administrators, school psychologists, and related services personnel. The purpose of the IEP team is to ensure accurate identification of the student's academic, social, and vocational needs. Moreover, the team is charged with creating an educational program that meets these needs. It should be noted that there is nothing in IDEA that prevents a child from receiving both special education services and gifted education services. Nevertheless, some school systems have interpreted the law in this manner. However, the inclusion of gifted students with learning disabilities in the reauthorization of the IDEA legislation in 2004 serves to clarify this population's protection under the law.

IDEA—School and/or school district responsibilities

Schools and school districts must fulfill certain requirements in order to be in compliance with the law. Schools must develop special education programs that permit twice-exceptional students to learn in the least restrictive learning environment. *Least restrictive* is defined as an educational placement that gives the student an opportunity to have the greatest amount of contact with peers while still meeting the student's individual needs. For twice-exceptional students, this means participating in gifted education programming in addition to receiving special education services. Specific school responsibilities include:

- identify and evaluate students who could qualify for special services under IDEA;
- develop, review, and revise IEPs, and initiate and conduct meetings;
- ensure that students are educated with their nondisabled peers to the fullest extent feasible;
- maintain confidentiality of student records;
- establish and implement procedural safeguards that ensure parents or guardians are equal participants in the special education process;

- provide technological devices and services when applicable; and
- provide the state a description of the personnel they will need to ensure a free and appropriate public education is provided to all students with disabilities (IDEA, 2004; Yell, 1998).

IDEA—Parent or guardian responsibilities

The biggest responsibility for the parent or guardian is to be an informed advocate for his or her twice-exceptional child. In many instances, the IEP team will seek to remediate the disability and neglect the gift. The parents or guardians must make sure that services are provided to address the child's abilities in addition to their disabilities. A parent or guardian's role in the process is to:

- actively participate in IEP meetings,
- advocate for appropriate programming,
- share information about student's strengths and weaknesses,
- assist in developing measurable goals and objectives, and
- provide support at home (Sevier County Department of Education, 2004a; Siegle, 2004).

IDEA—Student responsibilities

As gifted students with disabilities matriculate through school, they need to assume responsibility for their future. One way they can begin to take control over their future is by participating in the IEP process. This participation empowers students and allows them to practice advocating for themselves. A student's role is to:

- actively participate in the IEP process;
- communicate educational and personal concerns to the IEP team;
- cooperate with teachers, parents, and school administrators; and
- help to design measurable goals and objectives (IDEA, 2004; Sevier County Department of Education, 2004a; Siegle, 2004).

Developing IEPs that effectively meet the needs of gifted students with disabilities can be a difficult process. Making sure that appropriate goals and objectives are written can be time-consuming and tedious. If parents, teachers, and students have an open and collaborative relationship, the team will develop an effective IEP that meets the child's needs.

Scenario

Julie: A gifted student with a learning disability

Julie was identified for her school's gifted program in the third grade with an IQ over 135. Unfortunately, Julie's academic performance did not meet her intellectual ability. Although she performed above grade level for most subjects, she always struggled with mathematics. Initially, her third grade teacher felt that Julie needed to try harder in mathematics, so he arranged a conference with Julie's parents. During the conference, her teacher discovered that Julie studiously practiced math.

Based on the discussions at the parent conference, it was agreed that Julie needed to be referred to a support team. The team (including her parents) designed a few interventions, such as incorporating the use of multisensory instructional materials and computer programs for drill and practice. The interventions were implemented in all classrooms and reinforced at home. After 8 weeks, Julie's math achievement improved, but it did not reach the average level of her peers. Thus, the support team wrote an IEP for Julie.

It was determined that Julie's least restrictive environment was the general classroom for all subjects except mathematics. For math instruction, Julie met in a resource room with a special education teacher who provided remedial math instruction and taught Julie coping strategies to help compensate for her learning disability. As dictated by law, Julie's situation will be reviewed in a year.

General Characteristics of Gifted Students
With Learning Disabilities

Twice-exceptional students have a unique combination of characteristics. In truth, they possess some characteristics of both gifted and learning disabled individuals. However, the combination of these characteristics makes them a distinctive population that warrants specific individualized programming. Creating an absolute list of all the characteristics associated with gifted students with learning disabilities is not feasible; thus, the information presented here is generalized. In most cases, these students lack scholastic confidence because they struggle with basic academic skills such as organization, study skills, grapho-motor speed, perceptual scanning, sequencing, and metacognition (Baum, 1990). Table 1 highlights some of the common characteristics often associated with twice exceptional students across intellectual, academic, and social-emotional domains. While they have many characteristics of an individual with a learning disability, twice-exceptional students also possess characteristics of typically developing gifted children. In fact, gifted students with learning disabilities possess many strong intellectual skills that are not seen in typical students with learning disabilities alone. In addition to possessing precocious abstract reasoning skills, gifted students who have a learning disability

Table 1
General Characteristics of Gifted Students With Learning Disabilities

Intellectual Strengths (Lidz, 2002)	Academic Skill Deficiencies (Baum, 1990)	Social-Emotional Concerns (Beckley, 1998)
Advanced abstract reasoning skills	Low scholastic confidence	Aggression
Ability to make astute generalizations	Poor organizational and study skills	Anxiety
Quick conceptualization of ideas	Lack of graphomotor speed	Defensive
Enjoyment in solving novel tasks autonomously	Difficulty with sequencing	Disruptive in class
Precocious intellectual ability	Problems with metacognition	Low self-esteem

Note. Information compiled from Baum (1990), Beckley (1998), Lidz (2002).

are able to make astute generalizations, conceptualize ideas quickly, possess advanced abstract reasoning skills, and enjoy solving novel tasks autonomously (Lidz, 2002).

As a result of these paradoxical characteristics, gifted students with learning disabilities tend to have social-emotional issues that must be attended to such as aggression, anxiety, defensiveness, disruption in class, inability to stay on task, and poor self-esteem (Beckley, 1998). The implications of these social-emotional issues are addressed later.

By and large, students with learning disabilities—even those who are gifted—have difficulty internalizing and articulating information (Bergert, 2000). Certainly any child may have difficulty with one or more academic skills from time to time, yet for gifted children with learning disabilities, these problems persist over a significant period of time. Unfortunately, the combinations of these characteristics tend to have a negative impact on academic performance and are often frustrating for students. Thus, teachers, parents, and students need to be conscious of the characteristics of twice-exceptional individuals so they can design appropriate intervention strategies.

In order to minimize frustration and maximize performance, teachers and parents must create programming that harnesses gifts while prescribing strategies that diminish the effects of weaknesses. Far too often, there is the tendency to focus on the child's weaknesses. However, if students receive appropriate programming, they will learn how to effectively utilize their strengths to compensate for their weaknesses.

Tips for Teachers

Due to their dichotomous characteristics, teaching gifted students with learning disabilities can be challenging. However, there are many research-based strategies that teachers can employ that will minimize teacher/parent/student frustration and maximize student potential. Whether teaching to a student's strengths and learning styles or maintaining constant communication with parents, the tips listed below will facilitate student learning.

1. *Identify the student's strengths and weaknesses.* Fortunately, establishing the student's strengths and weaknesses is not as difficult as it may seem. A direct way of accomplishing this goal is to ask the student in what areas he feels he is strongest and weakest (See Appendix C for an example of an ability questionnaire). Too often, adults meet to discuss a student without including input from the student. The questions in Appendix C allow the student to express his or her feelings about school and provide teachers with a guide to follow when creating interventions and accommodations to implement in the classroom. In addition, teachers must ask for a developmental his-

tory of the child. This will serve to demonstrate the skills in which the student excels. The teacher will then be able to create learning activities that focus on the student's strengths.

2. *Identify a student's learning style and teach to that learning style* (Winebrenner, 2003). Many times, teachers only teach to their own learning style. This practice limits the opportunities for gifted students with learning disabilities who do not share the same learning style as the teacher.

Designing activities centered on the student's preferred learning style allows children to utilize their giftedness. In turn, they will feel more comfortable and confident in completing schoolwork. It is important to focus on students' gifts in order to build their self-esteem. Additionally, it affords twice-exceptional children the opportunity to use their gifts to compensate for their weaknesses.

3. *Teach organizational skills* (Cline & Schwartz, 1999; Swanson, 2001; Winebrenner, 2002). Not only do these students tend to have poor organizational skills with their physical space, but they also have poor mental organizational skills. Thus, teachers need to address both issues. Often, twice-exceptional students unsuccessfully complete assignments because they either lose the assignment or do not know when it is due.

Students must be taught how to organize a notebook, desk, book bag, and locker (Winebrenner, 2003). Learning organizational skills will help improve the frequency and accuracy of completed assignments. However, it is important that students assume responsibility for keeping their physical space organized.

Students must also be taught how to organize their mental space. Teachers should incorporate advanced organizers to improve mental organization. These tools allow students to apply prior knowledge to what they are currently learning. Examples of advanced organizers include K-W-L (what you Know, Want to know, and have Learned) charts, Venn diagrams, and concept mapping (Swanson, 2001).

4. *Collaborate with other teachers.* Collaboration must exist

among the special education, regular education, and gifted education teachers to ensure that all are working to meet the goals and objectives of the student's IEP. Moreover, these teachers must be willing to communicate with one another, discuss the student's progress in each classroom, and share effective instructional strategies (Winebrenner, 2002).

In addition, teachers must discuss what objectives are being taught in each classroom so they can align instruction across subjects. This approach assists students in making connections between disciplines and ultimately helps them use their strengths to compensate for their weaknesses. It will also help teachers better address the needs of the twice-exceptional student.

5. *Communicate with parents.* In order for any intervention plan to be successful, consistency between the school and home must exist. The skills being emphasized at school must also be stressed at home. To facilitate school-to-home cohesion, communication sheets should be sent home on a weekly basis. Teachers must expect the communication sheet to be returned in a timely fashion. However, it should be the student's responsibility to get the sheets completed, signed, and returned. If the sheets are not returned, there must be consequences both at school and home (see Appendix D for an example of a home-to-school form).

6. *Break large tasks into several small steps.* Swanson (2001) suggests that lengthy assignments be broken into several small steps. Not only will this help to reinforce specific skills, but it also allows twice-exceptional students to monitor their own progress.

7. *Provide peer modeling.* One proven method for helping twice-exceptional students learn coping strategies is peer modeling (Swanson, 2001). Through this strategy, non-learning-disabled peers model proper approaches to learning. This approach permits twice-exceptional students to see how a fellow student might implement learning strategies.

Practical Tips for the Home

Successfully parenting a twice-exceptional child requires a structured home environment and involvement in the child's daily life. In addition to assisting with schoolwork, parents of gifted students with learning disabilities must communicate with school officials, be knowledgeable about school law, and involve the child in extracurricular activities. The following tips will not only improve scholastic achievement but also will promote lifelong academic skills.

1. *Offer assistance with schoolwork.* Learning to use strengths to overcome weaknesses is a frustrating journey. Twice-exceptional children need to realize they are not alone. Parents must be willing to assist their children with academic work and help promote social-emotional strength (Baum, 1990).

A specific work area should be established at home where the student and parent can work on school assignments together. Working in this area will help establish a bond with the child and reinforce the notion that overcoming the disability is a team effort. Additionally, the parent and twice-exceptional child need to establish a time of the day to meet. During this period, the child should be allowed to discuss what is happening at school. Not only will this serve as a way to monitor the child's academic progress, but it also will allow the parent to monitor the child's frustration level.

2. *Involve the child in extracurricular activities.* Gifted students who have learning disabilities need to be in situations where they experience academic and social success. Furthermore, extracurricular activities are not limited to school-sponsored activities. There are a lot of community-related opportunities that will meet the interests of any child. It is important that these activities also meet the intellectual needs of the twice-exceptional child. Activities such as book clubs, chess clubs, scouting, community service groups, or sports teams provide a sense of accomplishment and enhance self-concept (Baum, 1990).

3. *Reinforce organizational skills.* One way to accomplish this goal is to create a family calendar and post it in a public place. The calendar will help the twice-exceptional child to learn proper time management skills. Include due dates for school assignments and family events. In addition, the child should create a personal calendar and post it in his or her bedroom or another private place. The child should be responsible for keeping the calendar up-to-date.

4. *Communicate with the child's teachers.* Although communication sheets are a meaningful medium, they are not enough. Parents need to schedule regular meetings with teachers. At these meetings, parents should ask questions about the student's performance. In addition, parents must ask teachers how to be of assistance at home. This will go a long way in promoting cooperation between the school and home (Winebrenner, 2003).

5. *Become educated about giftedness and learning disabilities.* Not only is it important to be familiar with special education law, but parents also must know appropriate steps to take if they are dissatisfied with the services the school is providing. Parents are the child's most important advocates, and in order to do a good job, they need to be knowledgeable.

6. *Provide one-on-one instruction.* Tutors are an excellent resource for creating individual attention. Tutoring sessions allow a trained educator to cater individualized learning activities and monitor student progress (Swanson, 2001). Tutors can coordinate the sessions with specific content being taught at school and then send reports to parents and teachers.

7. *Encourage self-monitoring.* One of the most important skills twice-exceptional students should learn is self-monitoring, because it has been proven to increase academic performance and engagement (Rock, 2005). By recording their study habits in a booklet, gifted students with learning disabilities can review how they study and identify effective behaviors.

The remaining sections in this guide will cover academic skill disabilities (reading, mathematics, and writing), developmental speech and language disabilities, and social-emotional issues. Although each disability manifests itself differently, the effect on the child, parent, and teacher is equally frustrating. Interventions need to boost self-efficacy, promote strengths, and provide coping strategies to compensate for disabilities.

Gifted Students With Reading Disabilities

Dyslexia is the most common reading disability for gifted students. Although dyslexia can affect a student's ability in mathematics, spelling, and speaking, the greatest affected area is reading. According to the International Dyslexia Association (2000), 15 to 20% of the general population has a reading disability, and of that group, 85% has dyslexia. While the information presented in this chapter is generalized to include all reading disabilities, many of the strategies have been proven effective for gifted students with dyslexia.

In general, gifted students with a reading disability have metacognitive difficulties that hinder reading prowess. They struggle with memorizing facts, reading comprehension, and organizing language (written and spoken). In addition, these students tend to confuse letters with similar sounds (i.e., *s* and *f*), confuse letters that look similar (i.e., *v* and *u*), switch letter placement within words, and reorder words within sentences (McGuire & Yewchuk, 1996). These difficulties make reading for understanding a complex endeavor.

Instructional strategies for gifted students with reading disabilities must promote comprehension. First, educators have to directly teach reading strategies that emphasize metacognitive control. Second, this population of students requires organizational and planning reading strategies. Interventions need to focus on strategic and structured reading strategies that enhance reading comprehension (Cooper, Ness, & Smith, 2004; McGuire & Yewchuk, 1996).

In order for these students to be academically successful, they need to learn an assortment of reading strategies ranging from letter and word recognition to comprehension and metacognition. Gifted students must first learn to correctly identify letters and sounds. Multisensory reading strategies are a proven method for increasing accuracy and allow twice-exceptional students to use their gifts to compensate for their reading disabilities. Next, gifted students with reading disabilities need to actively engage in reading through prediction and reflection.

Developing appropriate programming for gifted students with dyslexia requires cooperation among special education teachers, classroom teachers, and parents. Cooper et al. (2004) suggest regularly scheduled meetings among these individuals. The discussions should focus on educational and self-esteem issues that meet the student's unique needs. Programming suggestions include: (a) allowing the student to remain in the general classroom for most disciplines, (b) requiring special education services for disciplines where the student is performing below grade level, and (c) providing gifted education instruction for areas of precocious talent (Cooper et al.). These strategies will enable gifted students with a reading disability to access background knowledge and increase textual understanding. The tips below provide greater detail.

Scenario

Jennifer: A gifted student with a reading disability

Jennifer is a high school junior who was recently identified as gifted and diagnosed with a reading disability. Throughout her schooling, Jennifer was an average student who usually completed class assignments and homework on time. She struggled with reading comprehension but demonstrated satisfactory performance on tests and projects. Jennifer did not realize that her struggles with reading were abnormal. She simply thought that she just wasn't as bright as her peers.

At the beginning of her junior year, Jennifer's history teacher noticed a curious problem. During class discussions, Jennifer was able to orally summarize class lectures. In addition, she had a precocious ability to recall prior knowledge and synthesize information; however, Jennifer only earned C's on the exams. She particularly struggled with questions that assessed information from out-of-class readings. Concerned that Jennifer might have a reading disability, the teacher referred Jennifer for testing. The results of the testing revealed that Jennifer not only had a reading disability, but also had an IQ over 130. While Jennifer's reading disability had negatively impacted her academics, her high IQ allowed Jennifer to compensate for the disability.

Because she was performing as well as average students, a teacher support team designed a 504 plan that permitted Jennifer to go to a resource room to teach her how to use proper reading strategies (e.g., advanced organizers, Think Alongs, and assistive technologies) that enabled her to maximize her potential. In addition, the team (which included Jennifer) began looking into transition services so that Jennifer could utilize appropriate services at a post-secondary institution.

Tips for Teachers

Teaching gifted students with a reading disability requires teachers to incorporate a range of strategies. Some of these approaches access a student's prior knowledge while others help organize the reading process. The following tips are designed to teach twice-exceptional students reading fundamentals that allow them to be more efficient and effective readers.

1. Utilize strategies that incorporate a multisensory approach. One such strategy is known as the Orton-Gillingham (Herold, 2003) method of reading instruction. This tactic, developed by Dr. Samuel T. Orton and educator Anna Gillingham, accesses multiple senses through audio, visual, and kinesthetic learning activities. Gifted students with a reading disability need to utilize all of their senses when reading because it helps establish multiple memory patterns in the brain (Herold). Incorporating this strategy with twice-exceptional students also assists them in learning basic reading strategies and developing advanced comprehension skills.

Through the Orton-Gilllingham method, students are first taught the basic structure of language. In the beginning they learn consonant and vowel sounds, then they move on to the blending sounds such as digraphs and diphthongs. Next, twice-exceptional children are taught how to sound out syllables. Simultaneously, they learn how to write these same letters and syllables (Academy of Orton-Gillingham Practitioners and Educators, 2004). As students become more proficient with pronouncing and writing these basic elements, they move onto individual words, phrases, and finally, entire sentences. Once the process is mastered, gifted students can begin to develop comprehension skills and utilize their precocious intellectual talents.

2. Incorporate strategies that access the student's prior knowledge. Background knowledge influences an individual's ability to construct new meaning and provides a purpose for reading. Gifted students with reading disabilities must be able to combine old knowledge with new knowledge. Learning these skills will enable them to become independent readers.

There are several strategic activities that teachers can introduce that will help these twice-exceptional students become independent readers. Cooper (2000) suggests the following two strategies: preview/predict strategies (e.g., story map prediction or review and self-question) and K-W-L organizers. The purpose of these strategies is to provide the student with an organized method for reading. Prior to reading, students skim the material and predict its content. Next, as students read, they are able to confirm or modify their expectations.

3. *Incorporate Think Alongs or Think Aloud strategies.* These strategies directly teach students that thinking occurs when individuals are performing a process or a task. In addition, they aid students in learning the reading process (Cooper, 2000).

Examples of Think Alongs include: Plot Relationship Charts, Question Answer Relationships (QARs), and Directed Reading-Thinking Activities (DRTA). These strategies have been proven to help students become strategic readers (Jongsma, 1999/2000). The DRTA approach requires students to read the title, headings, and short passages of a particular reading selection and make predictions as to the plot, theme, events, and conclusion. After reading, students go back and check the accuracy of their predictions and correct any inaccuracies. One example of this approach is SCAN and RUN (Salembier, 1999; see Appendix E for an example). According to Salembier, this approach provides students with the necessary skills to monitor understanding before, during, and after reading.

4. *Make accommodations for twice-exceptional students.* In order to help this population maximize their potential, teachers should consider allowing additional time for reading or classroom assignments. Moreover, teachers can shorten the length of homework or projects (Winebrenner, 2003).

There are also assistive technologies that can be utilized. Twice-exceptional students should be allowed to use electronic recording devices to record classroom discussions. Additionally, teachers should permit these students to use books on tape as an aid—not a substitute to the texts they are reading. The books on tape will still provide opportunities for comprehension without eliminating the use of classical works of literature.

5. *Identify student interests and provide readings that meet them.* A common characteristic of gifted students is high motivation in

areas of interest. Combining specific reading comprehension strategies with interest-centered reading is a well-established practice. First, gifted students with reading disabilities will be more willing to engage in reading. Second, these students will be more apt to participate in a discussion about the reading (Winebrenner, 2003).

Tips for Parents

On a daily basis, there are numerous intervention opportunities for parents of gifted students with a reading disability. Whether modeling good habits, reinforcing strategies taught in school, or having a family book club, parents of twice-exceptional children can help promote proper reading habits. These tips will help parents create a nurturing reading environment at home.

1. *Reinforce strategies taught in school.* In order to be successful readers, these twice-exceptional students must realize that reading skills learned in school are transferable to the real world. Thus, parents must work with their child at home. Parents must be willing to aid the child with homework assignments. Children should read aloud as they complete homework assignments. This will help parents to better understand their child's reading strengths and weaknesses (Shaywitz & Shaywitz, 2004; U.S. Department of Education, 2002).

In addition, parents must require their twice-exceptional child to create and complete a summer reading list. This will help to ensure that the reading strategies learned during the school year are not forgotten during the summer months. Furthermore, summer is a wonderful time for twice-exceptional children to read about topics of interest (U.S. Department of Education, 2002).

2. *Model reading habits.* It is important for a gifted child with dyslexia to see reading as a fundamental aspect of everyday life. Read articles in the newspaper and discuss their main ideas. Not only will this provide parents with a method for informally

evaluating their child's progress, but it also reinforces the importance of everyday reading skills (U.S. Department of Education, 2002).

Another activity is for families to institute a "Family Book Club." Bimonthly, each family member could discuss a book. Try making this a special event by discussing the book over a family prepared dinner or an afternoon family picnic. The setting should be relaxing and fun.

3. *Take advantage of computer programs focusing on reading.* These products are designed to promote good reading skills and provide interventions for various skill deficiencies. Moreover, many of these programs are interactive, whereby students can write their own stories and intermingle with the story's main characters. There are numerous reading software programs readily available for gifted children with reading disabilities (Bull, 2003; U.S. Department of Education, 2002).

4. *Provide one-on-one help when needed.* Although parents can provide such assistance, another great source of one-on-one help is tutors. Many qualified tutors are retired teachers who have experience with teaching students with reading difficulties. Moreover, these individuals will be able to monitor student progress and adjust strategies to meet the twice-exceptional child's needs (Bull, 2003).

5. *Utilize the public library.* Many libraries have book clubs and reading incentive programs. Gifted children with reading disabilities should obtain a library card. This act alone will help empower the child and give them a feeling of reading ownership (U.S. Department of Education, 2002).

6. *Provide constant and sustained opportunities to practice reading.* Gifted students with reading disabilities must constantly practice reading strategies they have learned. Shaywitz and Shaywitz (2004) stress that these students must spend time practicing their reading strategies each day. Whether parents are reading with their child or reinforcing reading strategies

learned at school, they should help their child establish a daily reading time. Only through focused attention to reading basics will these twice-exceptional students become fluent readers (Shaywitz & Shaywitz).

7. *Participate in a support group.* There are organizations that offer support groups for parents of children with reading disabilities. The benefits of such groups range from finding emotional support to identifying proven intervention strategies (Bull, 2003).

In order to maximize their potential, gifted students with reading disabilities must learn how to use their intellectual strengths to compensate for their reading difficulties. These students must realize they will always have a reading disability, for no interventions exist that can completely eliminate it. However, instructional strategies can be developed that empower these students and enable them to become lifelong autonomous readers.

Practical Strategies for Gifted Students
With a Mathematics Disability

The term *dyscalculia* refers to a person who has a specific mathematics learning disability (Newman, 1998). Although dyscalculia can manifest itself in a variety of forms, all of which entail difficulty in solving mathematical problems, 20 to 30% of individuals with this disability have difficulties with both reading and mathematics. According to Geary (1999), between 6 and 7% of school children have some form of mathematics disability. The information presented in this chapter focuses on mathematical strategies that can be incorporated at school and home. Although some of the activities focus on remedial strategies, it is imperative that gifted students with dyscalculia receive intellectually challenging instruction. In order to accomplish this goal, teachers and parents must work together to identify specific strengths and weaknesses.

Students who are gifted and have a mathematics learning disability demonstrate only modest knowledge of their cognitive strategies and even less of their metacognitive strategies (Montague, 1991). Moreover, they lack proficient visual perceptual deficiencies (Adler, 2001). In other words, they have difficulties with mentally organizing mathematic operational procedures. They tend to reverse numbers and struggle to remember the meaning of mathematical symbols.

Instructionally speaking, this population of twice-exceptional students requires interventions that focus on basic mathematical procedures and improving mathematical metacognitive skills. However, this does not mean they are unable to perform complex mathematical equations. They simply need strategies to help them mentally organize all the information.

Aside from these instructional options, teachers must be mindful of students' frustration level. These students need to experience success and receive positive reinforcement from their instructional program in order to develop self-assurance and a strong self-efficacy (Newman, 1998).

Scenario

Joshua: A gifted student with a mathematics disability

Joshua is a freshman in high school who was diagnosed with a mathematics disability in the third grade. His initial IEP required that he spend most of his day in the general education classroom and only go to the resource room for math instruction. The interventions included utilizing step-by-step procedures for solving all math problems, exchanging communication sheets between Joshua's teachers and his parents, and reducing the number of math problems on his tests. Although Joshua matriculated through school with his age peers, he was not identified as gifted until the eighth grade.

During the eighth grade, Joshua's science fair project investigated the effects that laundry detergents and water temperature have on the fading of colors in various types of fabrics. Using the organizational skills that he learned from his mathematics resource teacher, he determined which laundry detergents are harsher on specific types of fabrics. The hard work paid off for Joshua, as he won third place at the state science fair. In addition, his guidance counselor suggested that Joshua take Advanced Placement (AP) science classes in high school.

Intrigued that Joshua had performed so well at the science fair, his parents asked the school to reevaluate his IQ. The school psychometrist administered a verbal measure of intelligence, which allowed Joshua to maximize his skills. As a result of the reevaluation, it was determined that he had an IQ over 125. Not only did Joshua sign up for AP science classes, but he also took AP history and English classes. In addition, he continued to receive individualized mathematical instruction with a resource teacher.

Tips for Teachers

Gifted students with a mathematics disability require organized, well-structured coping strategies to help them compensate for their weaknesses. By incorporating multisensory activities and computer software programs, teachers can facilitate the learning process and provide twice-exceptional students proven approaches to solving mathematical problems.

1. *Provide an organized strategy for completing math problems.* This structure enables students to access the required prior knowledge needed to solve the current problem. Teachers must provide twice-exceptional students with a strategic plan that takes advantage of these students' strengths.

The MATHCOUNTS Foundation (2004) proposes the following four-step strategy be taught to all students, including gifted individuals with mathematics disabilities:

1. Find out—Read the problem and determine what is known and unknown. Access prior knowledge to determine how similar problems were solved.
2. Choose a strategy—List strategies you know and then eliminate the ones that will not help to solve the problem. Select the most appropriate strategy.
3. Solve it—Work the problem.

4. Look back—Read the original problem again to
    determine if your solution answers the question.

These four steps are appropriate for twice-exceptional students, because they provide them with a blueprint for solving
math problems, whether they are trying to solve simple mathematical problems or complex algebraic equations.

  2. *Incorporate a multisensory approach* (Newman, 1997). A
multisensory approach provides gifted disabled students with
stronger associative memories from which they can mentally
store and retrieve information. Newman discusses a three-step
process to help students memorize the basics:
  1. Verbalize and visualize—Students must state and pic-
      ture the facts. This step helps provide a storage area in
      the brain. This step should be repeated four times
      before moving on to the next step.
  2. Sky writing—Students should write in the air as they
      state the facts. In addition to stating and sky writing the
      facts, students should watch themselves. This step
      teaches the student how to retrieve the mentally stored
      information. Again, this step should be repeated four
      times.
  3. Tracing—Students should trace the information in
      their palms or on the desktop. This step helps to teach
      the student how to express the information. Once
      again, it should be repeated four times.

  3. *Make use of software programs designed to help students with
mathematics learning disabilities.* According to Babbit (1999),
gifted students with mathematics disabilities who make use of
software programs tend to stay on task longer, have greater
growth in math skills, and find learning more enjoyable than
those who do not.
  It is important to note that not all programs are effective.
Teachers who decide to incorporate software programs to aid
twice-exceptional students must be willing to review and evaluate them prior to using them as an instructional aid. When

evaluating the programs, teachers should look for software that matches strategies being used in the classroom, provides feedback to the student and teacher, does not muddle the screen with unnecessary graphics, and allows the user to adjust the program's settings.

4. *Utilize the student's strengths in other areas.* One method for accessing those strengths is to teach these twice-exceptional students how to draw a picture of the problem. According to the MATHCOUNTS Foundation (2004), this approach is appropriate for twice-exceptional students because it permits them to utilize additional mental processes. This type of strategy is good for completing mapping, geometry, and graphing problems.

5. *Allow students to use graph paper as opposed to regular notebook paper.* This allows gifted students with dyscalculia to write each digit in a separate box on the grid. This will aid students in keeping numbers aligned when working mathematical problems.

Tips for Parents

These twice-exceptional students require an encouraging home environment that reinforces strategies learned in school. Parents can promote math achievement by assisting with math homework, previewing the next day's lesson, and utilizing assistive technologies. It is important to create a home environment that is rich in authentic mathematical experiences.

1. *Help students visualize how math facts translate to other situations.* Fortunately, on a daily basis there are countless opportunities where twice-exceptional children can utilize math skills in authentic situations. Newman (1998) suggests that parents allow their child to help balance the checkbook, plan a weekly grocery shopping budget, or even figure change when paying for a meal.

Twice-exceptional children who participate in these activities become more confident in their math skills. Not only do these activities reinforce classroom instruction, but they also provide students with real life experience on which to draw. Furthermore, it affords parents with opportunities to mathematically interact with their child and to informally evaluate the child's development.

2. *Provide as many authentic learning situations as possible.* Projects around the house are a great way for gifted students with a mathematics learning disability to utilize classroom concepts. Examples of projects that require math include painting a room, landscaping, and cooking.

3. *Preview the next day's math lesson.* This tip helps the child preestablish connections to prior knowledge. Parents should encourage the child to write questions for the teacher and ask those questions during math class. This type of preparation transforms class lectures into review sessions and will increase productivity (Keller, 2004).

4. *Utilize assistive technologies.* Before rushing out to purchase expensive hardware and software, parents must evaluate the item's effectiveness. Consult the child's teachers to determine compatibility of these items and classroom instruction (Keller, 2004).

5. *Demonstrate patience.* Often, mathematics is difficult for students without a disabling condition, but for gifted students with a mathematics disability heightened levels of anxiety may exist. In addition to incorporating the tips mentioned above, parents must be supportive and understanding.

Dysgraphia is a term used to describe students who have difficulties articulating themselves through written language. Although gifted students have been identified with dysgraphia and are absent of any other learning disability, they generally are diagnosed as being dysgraphic and dyslexic. In order to accurately diagnose dysgraphia, it is important to assess an individual's visual memory, fine motor skills, visual perceptual skills, and ability to graphically reproduce information (Mather, 2003).

Gifted students with dysgraphia have difficulties with lower-level skills such as fine-motor, orthographic-motor integration, and letter-sound correspondences in word recognition. Moreover, these twice-exceptional students also experience troubles with higher-level skills such as language processing and metacognition (Yates, Berninger, & Abbott, 1995). In addition to writing difficulties, many gifted students have a spelling disability. According to Stringer, Morton, and Bonikowski (1999), characteristics of gifted students with spelling disabilities include low phonological knowledge, low motor control, low ability to visualize a word, and low auditory and visual memory skills.

Yates et al. (1995) report some significant implications for teachers of gifted students with specific writing disabilities. Aside from having difficulty with transferring thoughts to the written word, these students experience text generation or writing troubles. Many times their writing abilities may be compromised by their transcription deficiencies. Moreover, this population of gifted students becomes easily frustrated, experiences low self-esteem, and displays a low motivation to engage in writing. Finally, gifted, writing disabled students require interventions that specifically address the low-level aspects of the disability without compromising instruction that satisfies their precocious intellectual abilities.

Scenario

Robert: A gifted student with a writing disability

Robert is a seventh grader who was diagnosed with a writing disability in the fifth grade. He was identified for the district's gifted program in the second grade based primarily on his high verbal scores. Although he is a strong reader and has excellent oral language skills, he struggles with assignments that require extended writing. While Robert can verbally demonstrate comprehension of long complex readings, he finds it difficult to write down his thoughts.

In the fourth grade, Robert's grades in writing started to suffer as assignments began focusing on writing composition. Robert's handwriting had always been sloppy, but now it appeared as though his written ideas were disorganized and incomplete. Concerned by changes in Robert's academic performance, his parents had the school test Robert for a learning disability. The results of the test indicated that Robert had dysgraphia.

In an attempt to provide appropriate programming for Robert, his parents met with general classroom teachers, special education teachers, and the gifted education teacher.

As a group, they developed an IEP for Robert. As a result, Robert spent most of the day in his general education classroom, went to a resource room for help with his writing deficiencies, and continued to participate in his gifted class. Daily, Robert carried an assignment sheet with him so that all teachers knew what objectives were being taught in other classrooms. The assignment sheet also went home with Robert so that his parents could monitor and reinforce strategies taught in school.

Tips for Teachers

Teaching gifted students with dysgraphia is difficult because students can orally explain their thoughts better than writing them. To help twice-exceptional children compensate for their disability, teachers can adjust the length of writing assignments, utilize assistive technologies, and develop graphic organizers. The following tips are designed to provide students with systematic coping strategies.

1. *Develop a strategic plan to assist students in conveying their ideas into writing.* Writing is an important skill required by any occupation. In order for twice-exceptional students to maximize their potential, they must be able to strategically organize and write their ideas. Keller (2004) promotes the POWER method as an effective strategy. The POWER method involves the following steps:

- plan the writing,
- organize thoughts and ideas,
- write the essay,
- edit the work, and
- revise the draft and create the final draft.

This method is appropriate for twice-exceptional students because it provides a strategic plan that can be employed with any writing assignment. Not only is the acronym easy to remember, but the steps are also simple to follow.

2. *Implement graphic organizers.* This strategy is appropriate for gifted students with dysgraphia for two reasons: It teaches twice-exceptional students how to organize their ideas, and it serves as a visual reference enabling students to see their thoughts (Keller, 2004). For this population, getting ideas from the brain to paper is difficult. This strategy teaches gifted students with dysgraphia how to brainstorm.

3. *Breakup long-term writing assignments into several mini-assignments.* For example, have separate deadlines for selecting a topic, gathering resources, completing an outline, writing a rough draft, and revising and writing a final draft. It is best to discuss possible alterations to the above suggestions with the student. However, establishing intermittent deadlines is beneficial to twice-exceptional students because it helps them to organize their ideas and work (Richards, 1999).

4. *Allow gifted students to use either print or cursive writing styles.* Many gifted students with dysgraphia struggle with the physical aspect of writing. These students should be encouraged to use the cursive writing style. Richards (1999) indicates this writing style is easier because it is a smoother movement. The natural flow of cursive is less taxing on the muscles. However many gifted students with dysgraphia, especially those who have already learned to write, find it easier to use the print writing style. The determining factor should be the writing style that is most legible.

5. *Utilize assistive technology devices.* Computers eliminate twice-exceptional students' needs to manually write down their ideas. There are several computer software programs that allow students to create graphic organizers and plan writing assignments. Moreover, many word processing programs help students check their grammar and spelling (Richards, 1999).

Another assistive technology device that can be integrated into the classroom is the tape recorder. Often, twice-exceptional students come up with wonderful ideas only to forget them. According to Keller (2004), tape recorders allow gifted students with dysgraphia to record their ideas so they can be revisited later.

Tips for Parents

Whether seeking assistance from an occupational therapist or providing access to word processing programs, parents can help their twice-exceptional child develop coping strategies to overcome dysgraphia. These at-home tips will encourage children to become more proficient writers.

1. *Use appropriate paper to increase writing proficiency.* Keller (2004) suggests that parents insist their children use paper with raised lines. This type of paper helps to promote more legible handwriting and increases student productivity. Although this type of paper is most effective with younger twice-exceptional students, it is appropriate for individuals of all ages.

Notebook paper comes in a variety of line widths. Older children should be permitted to select the line width with which they feel most comfortable. Keller (2004) indicates that some students will use small writing to disguise their disability. Paper with wide lines will make it more difficult to hide these deficiencies.

2. *Help the child review class notes.* This tip will not only help the gifted student with dysgraphia to study, but it will also ensure that the student understands the information discussed in class. Moreover, it affords parents the opportunity to informally assess the child's progress. This tip should be implemented several times a week to guarantee comprehension.

3. *Seek therapy from an occupational therapist (OT).* Richards (1999) suggests that this therapist can help with fatigue, gross motor skills, and pencil grip. The OT will generally teach the student some hand exercises to counteract these issues.

4. *Encourage writing skills at home.* One way to meet this goal is for parents and the child to write letters to family and friends. This tip could be the basis for a "letter day" once a month. Letter writing among friends and family allows children to practice writing skills without academic pressure. To promote proper letter writing skills at home, encourage the child to organize his or her ideas before writing the letter. This strategy also helps reinforce skills learned at school.

5. *Provide access to word processing programs.* Richards (1999) suggests having the child practice typing at least 10 minutes a day. While there are numerous typing software programs, one effective method is to allow the child to have Instant Message conversations with friends. Not only will this help with typing skills, but it will also help to enhance the twice-exceptional child's written communication skills.

Spoken Language Disorders and Gifted Students

Language-based learning disabilities that interfere with age-appropriate reading, spelling, and writing are known as spoken language disorders. According to the American Speech-Language-Hearing Association (2003), 20% of students who received special education services during the 1998–1999 school year were treated for speech/language disorders. While this disorder does not impair an individual's intelligence, it does affect twice-exceptional students' abilities to express their knowledge. Gifted individuals with language learning disabilities tend to have receptive and expressive difficulties (Hayes & Norris, 1998).

Twice-exceptional students with poor receptive language skills lack appropriate listening comprehension abilities needed to understand oral language. This deficiency results in gaps in knowledge and difficulty with social situations. Gifted students with spoken language disorders do not have hearing impairments, rather their difficulties reside at a basic metacognitive level. These twice-exceptional students struggle with all forms of verbal instruction (Mather & Goldstein, 2001).

Scenario

Fredrick: A gifted student with a speech/language disorder

Fredrick was identified with a speech/language disorder at age 5 and immediately began seeing a speech-language pathologist. Although the speech/language disorder did not impede his academics, Fredrick did have a noticeable stutter. Academically, he far exceeded his classmates and demonstrated a precocious visual-spatial ability. This precocious ability led Fredrick's teacher to refer him for the school's gifted program.

At the end of the first grade, Fredrick was identified as gifted using an individualized nonverbal measure of intelligence. As he entered the second grade, Fredrick's parents insisted on a meeting with his teachers and speech-language pathologist. The discussion focused on how Fredrick's unique needs were going to be met in all classrooms.

Based on those meetings, the team decided that Fredrick would continue to receive therapy. In addition, Fredrick's gifted education teacher would require that he practice the speech language interventions in class, as well as utilize alternative means of communication to express himself. The parents agreed to reinforce speech/language interventions at home.

Tips for Teachers

Tips for teaching gifted students with speech/language disorders range from consulting a speech-language pathologist (SLP) to allowing students alternative means of expression. Teachers should create an accepting classroom environment that encourages twice-exceptional students.

1. *Collaborate with the speech-language pathologist.* Teachers need to provide the SLP with the objectives that are being

taught in the classrooms. Communication between teachers and the SLP is an important aspect of the twice-exceptional student's development. All parties must work together to ensure that the student's needs are being met (Hayes & Norris, 1998).

2. *Serve as a good speech role model and provide a classroom that encourages communication.* Gifted students with speech/language disorders will be hesitant to speak in class, thus it is imperative that the teacher provide a safe learning environment. One way is to create cooperative learning group activities. These small groups are not as intimidating and allow twice-exceptional students to fully express themselves (Mather & Goldstein, 2001).

3. *Find alternative means of communication that will allow students with speech/language disorders to express themselves* (Mather & Goldstein, 2001). In the classroom, the most common form of communication is speaking; however, it is not the only medium. The teacher must be willing to allow the student an opportunity to express his or her knowledge. Perhaps the twice-exceptional child could write down his or her answers. Or, rather than making a formal speech or presentation, the teacher could allow the student to demonstrate what was learned through the creation of a Web site.

Tips for Parents

Tips for parenting a gifted child with speech/language disorders range from creating a multisensory home environment to playing family word games. These proven tips not only promote phonological ability, but also build the child's confidence in his or her speaking ability.

1. *Seek assistance from speech-language pathologists.* Speech-language pathologists provide individual speech therapy and can coordinate services with school officials. For gifted students whose learning disability is caused by speech/language disorders, speech therapy has proven to be effective. In fact, after

receiving services, many of these students are able to fully compensate for the speech problem (Hayes, 1993).

2. *Develop oral language at home.* According to Learning Disabilities of America (1999), parents should enhance phonological ability by playing word games with their child. Examples of such games include rhyming words, drawing pictures, and having children orally create stories about pictures. In addition to enhancing phonics, these games also instill confidence to orally manipulate language.

3. *Create a home environment that stimulates all the senses.* Cicci (1995) insists that twice-exceptional children will develop greater language skills if they learn to utilize their senses. Exploration of objects through touching, smelling, tasting, seeing, and hearing permits these children to create more experiences to draw upon. Parents should sit with their children and ask them to describe the objects around them.

American schools are filled with a large population of children who are both gifted and learning disabled. In addition to academic and intellectual characteristics, twice-exceptional students have specific social-emotional needs that must be met. These students need to experience success, receive positive reinforcement, and develop appropriate social skills from their instructional program in order to develop self-assurance and a strong self-efficacy.

The information presented in this section focuses on the social-emotional characteristics of twice-exceptional children. Although the information is generalized to the entire gifted/learning disabled population, the suggested strategies are based on empirical research. Furthermore, these suggestions are not meant to substitute the services provided by trained and licensed psychologists. Rather, they are simple strategies intended to enhance self-efficacy in the classroom and at home.

Strop and Goldman (2002) assert that twice-exceptional students exhibit the following social-emotional characteristics: "(a) anger, (b) fear of failure, (c) fear of success, (d) low self-esteem, and (e) strong need of control" (p. 28). Interestingly, these characteristics reflect a pessimistic self-concept that tends to manifest into poor academic performance. In fact, Olenchak and Reis (2002) report that many twice-exceptional students describe their school experiences in a gloomy and unfavorable light.

In order to enhance self-efficacy, it is important that instructional strategies spotlight the student's strengths, interests, and superior intellectual capacities (Beckley, 1998). Many of the instructional strategies mentioned in earlier chapters are designed to meet these needs. The tips that follow have proven to be effective in enabling gifted students with learning disabilities to develop the required skills to successfully function in the world.

Tips for Teachers

Teachers must consider the social-emotional effects the classroom environment has on twice-exceptional students. Classrooms that provide a variety of educational opportunities that match students' unique needs allow them to be educationally and socially successful.

1. *Provide instruction that is intellectually challenging in a stimulating learning environment.* This strategy is appropriate for enhancing the social-emotional level of twice-exceptional students because it allows students to utilize their strengths. In essence, teachers need to create learning experiences that permit twice-exceptional students to be successful. In fact, Hua and Coleman (2002) insist that successful experiences boost self-esteem, instill confidence, and enhance self-efficacy.

2. *Establish mentorship programs* (Olenchak & Reis, 2002). These programs are appropriate for gifted students with learning disabilities and provide the opportunity for students to learn from adults who care about their social, emotional, and academic progress. By placing these students in real-world situations, they are free to explore the endless possibilities of their talents. Moreover, a mentorship is a wonderful educational experience for twice-exceptional students because it builds self-esteem and confidence.

3. *Allow twice-exceptional students to experience success.* Baum, Owen, and Dixon (1991) discuss several proven strategies that enable gifted students with learning disabilities to be successful. These strategies include, but are not limited to, designing cooperative learning group activities, utilizing peer tutoring, dividing large assignments into several small assignments, and using praise as a reinforcer (Baum et al.). All of these strategies help promote self-efficacy and confidence.

Tips for Parents

A positive, reassuring home environment is key to maximizing the potential of twice-exceptional students. In addition to getting children involved in extracurricular activities, parents must spend time listening to their child's daily academic and social frustrations.

1. *Involve the child in after-school activities that enhance self-efficacy* (Olenchak & Reis, 2002). Whether participating in community clubs, sports teams, or academic associations, gifted students with learning disabilities often develop meaningful social relationships. Moreover, they learn how to maximize their strengths and compensate for their disabilities. It is important for parents to encourage their twice-exceptional child to engage in after-school programs. This population of children requires opportunities that highlight their strengths.

2. *Seek out group therapy programs that enhance self-esteem.* Olenchak and Reis (2002) assert that twice-exceptional children benefit from programs that include gifted/learning disabled peers. These situations are positive because they allow twice-exceptional children to establish relationships with individuals who share similar experiences. In addition, group counseling programs are led by experts with experience in counseling gifted students with learning disabilities.

3. *Allow children to discuss their frustrations.* Gifted students with learning disabilities face many frustrations at school and

home, with their peers and adults. In order to develop a positive self-esteem, twice-exceptional students must be able to discuss their frustrations with their parents. Parents must sit down with their children and discuss the day's events. A perfect opportunity to meet this goal is the dinner table. This family time allows twice-exceptional children to share their feelings and emotions. It also permits parents to informally evaluate their child's emotional state.

My experiences with twice-exceptional students have been as a teacher and researcher. In many ways, I have found this group of gifted students to be just like gifted, nondisabled students. They are intelligent, astute, and creative. They require individualized educational planning that focuses on strengths in such a fashion that permits their giftedness to shine.

In addition to lacking advanced social skills, I have found this group of students to be easily frustrated and disorganized. Twice-exceptional students require educational programming that allows them to be successful. They must learn how to utilize their strengths to compensate for their disabilities.

Educational institutions and parents must work with twice-exceptional students to establish curricular programs that are multidisciplinary in focus and use authentic forms of assessment. The key to maximizing the potential of gifted students with learning disabilities is early identification. Parents and teachers must be made aware of the characteristics of these students. Once properly identified, educators can create appropriate programs to address the needs of twice-exceptional students.

Web Sites

All Kinds of Minds
http://www.allkindsofminds.org

A private, nonprofit institute, affiliated with the University of North Carolina at Chapel Hill that offers a powerful system of programs for helping children succeed. The site contains articles and ideas for dealing with certain types of abilities and is geared towards parents and educators.

Dyscalculia.org
http://dyscalculia.org

Provides numerous resources for parents and teachers. Whether looking for information about dyslexia, dyscalculia, or dysgraphia, this site is a good source.

LD-Online
http://ldonline.org

Contains information about serving students with learning disabilities. The site also has an entire section devoted to twice-exceptional students.

Schwab Learning
http://schwablearning.org

Provides resources to help kids with learning disorders and Attention-Deficit/Hyperactivity Disorder lead satisfying and productive lives. Information is available for parents that describe how to effectively advocate for their child.

Sevier County Board Of Education
http://www.slc.sevier.org

Provides users with a comprehensive explanation of IDEA and Section 504. Contains resources for both parents and teachers.

Organizations

American Speech-Language-Hearing Association
10801 Rockville Pike
Rockville, MD 20852
(800) 638-8255 (Toll-free)
(301) 897-5700 (TTY)
(301) 571-0457 (fax)
http://www.asha.org

Promotes the interests of and the highest quality services for professions in audiology, speech-language pathology, and speech and hearing science, and advocates for people with communication disabilities.

Association of Educational Therapists
1804 W. Burbank Boulevard.
Burbank, CA 91506
(800) 286-4267
(818) 843-7423 (fax)
http://www.aetonline.org

Contains information on upcoming events and a list of association publications.

The Council for Exceptional Children
1110 North Glebe Road, Ste. 300
Arlington, VA 22201-5704
(888) CEC-SPED
703-620-3660 (Local)
866-915-5000 (TTY: text only)
(703)-264-9494 (fax)
http://www.cec.sped.org

Contains information about professional development, articles from its publications, information about professional standards and public policies, and a bulletin board system.

Council for Learning Disabilities
P.O. Box 4014
Leesburg, VA 20177
(571) 258-1010
(571) 258-1011 (fax)
http://www.cldinternational.org

An international organization concerned about issues related to students with learning disabilities. Information about conferences and legislation are available on this site.

ERIC Clearinghouse on Disabilities and Gifted Education
2277 Research Boulevard, 6M
Rockville, MD 20850
(800) 328-0272
http://ericec.org

Gathers and disseminates professional literature, information, and resources on the education and development of individuals of all ages who have disabilities and who are gifted.

The International Dyslexia Association
Chester Building, Ste. 382
8600 LaSalle Road
Baltimore, MD 21286-2044
(410) 296-0232
(410) 321-5069 (fax)
http://www.interdys.org

Nonprofit organization dedicated to helping individuals with dyslexia, their families, and the communities that support them. The site is divided into sections for parents, college students, educators, children, teens, and adults. There are bulletin boards, information about dyslexia, public policy information, and research.

Learning Disabilities Association of America (LDA)
4156 Library Road
Pittsburgh, PA 15234-1349
(412) 341-1515
(412) 344-0224 (fax)
http://www.ldanatl.org

Promotes the advancement of education for learning disabled individuals. Furthermore, it supports individuals with learning disabilities, their families, and the professionals who work with them.

National Center for Learning Disabilities

381 Park Avenue South, Ste. 1401
New York, NY 10016
(212) 545-7510
(888) 575-7373 (Toll-free)
(212) 545-9665 (fax)
http://www.ld.org

Provides national leadership in support of children and adults with learning disabilities offering information, resources, and referral services. This site includes a lot of information about learning disabilities, tips for parents and teachers, legislative information, research news, and a resource locator.

Appendix A: Differences Between Section 504 and IDEA

Program Component	Section 504	IDEA
Type	A civil rights act	An education act and a civil rights act
Funding	Local funding	State/federal/local funding
Administration	Section 504 coordinator	Special education director
Service Tool	Accommodations	Individualized Education Program
Disabilities	Eligible disabilities under Section 504	Federal disability categories under IDEA
Parents	Should be involved in all team meetings	Should be involved in all team meetings
Procedural safeguards	Parent notice is required; consent is best practice	Parent notice and consent are required
Evaluation	Needed to decide eligibility and needed services under Section 504	Needed to decide eligibility and needed services under IDEA

Note. From *Section 504 Made Easy*, by Sevier County Board of Education, 2004b, Retrieved October 16, 2004, from http://www.slc.sevier.org/504easy. doc. Copyright ©2004 Sevier County Board of Education. Reprinted with permission.

Appendix B: Tips on Developing 504 Plans

Physical Accommodations	Instructional Accommodations	Behavioral Accommodations
Provide structured environment: • post schedules on board • post classroom rules • preferential seating (near teacher, between well-focused students, away from distractions) • organize workspace • use color codes	Repeat and simplify directions: • keep oral directions clear and simple • give examples • ask child to repeat back directions when possible • make eye contact • demonstrate	Use positive reinforcement: • positive verbal or written feedback • reward systems and incentives • give tasks that can be completed • private signals • role play situations • weekly individual time • conference opportunities
Provide private workspace: • quiet area for study • extra seat or table • standing work station • "time out" spot	Provide directions in written form: • on board • on worksheets • copied in assignment book by student and initialed by teacher	Be consistent: • with rewards and consequences • with posted rules
Provide learning centers: • reading corner • listening center • hands-on area	Individualize homework assignments: • reduce volume of work • break long-term assignments into manageable tasks • allow specified extended time without penalty for lateness • offer alternative assignments • provide extra set of texts at home	Promote leadership and accountability • assign jobs that can be performed well • "Student of the Week/Month" • provide responsibilities
	Use technological learning aides: • tape recorders • recorded lectures and assignments • computers • multi-sensory manipulatives	Set specific goals and reinforce them with incentives: • state tangible goals and timetable • reward system • incentives chart for work and behavior • student contracts
	Modified testing: • distraction free area • extended time	Communicate with parents, teachers, etc.: • letters • meetings • phone calls • use school staff for support

Appendix C: Student Strengths Inventory

Name: Date:

Answer the following questions to the best of your ability.

What do you do well?

What do you not do well?

What do you like the most about school?

What do you like least about school?

What academic skill would you most like to improve?

What social skill would you most like to improve?

Appendix D: Weekly Progress Report

_____'s Weekly Report.

Please read, sign, and return this report to school with your child. If you would like to discuss any part of the report with me, you can contact me at _____, between the hours of _____ and _____.

Teacher Initials

Comments   Objectives

_____ Completed all classroom assignments.

_____ Completed all homework assignments.

_____ Used class time wisely.

_____ Understood the concepts covered.

_____ Contributed to class discussions and
                                 activities.

_____ Behaved appropriately.

_____ Respected the rights of other students.

_____ Respected authority.

Note. From *Weekly Progress Report,* by Education World.com, 2003, Retrieved July 31, 2005, from http://www.educationworld.com/tools_templates/Weekly ProgressReports.doc. Copyright ©2003 by EducationWorld.com. Adapted with permission of the author.

Appendix E: SCAN & RUN

S = Survey headings and turn them into questions

"Survey headings" means scanning the title, headings, and subheadings of the text selection, and changing each into what, why, or how questions. This cue helps you identify key questions to be answered when you read the selection.

C = Capture the captions and visuals

"Capturing captions and visual clues" is the process of reading and trying to understand each caption or visual clue, and then asking yourself what the caption or visual clue means.

A = Attack boldface words

"Attacking boldface words" consists of reading highlighted words in the text selection and figuring out what each word means. Key vocabulary words are often boldfaced or underlined and found in the beginning of the selection or incorporated in the text. This cue may help you better understand the selection's main idea and details.

N = Note and read the chapter questions

"Note and read the chapter questions" means reading the questions at the end of the chapter before you read the selection. This cue helps you focus on answering the questions when you read.

R = Read and adjust speed

"Read and adjust speed" refers to changing your reading speed depending on the level of difficulty of the selection. This cue helps you slow down or speed up to better understand the meaning of the words in the text.

U = Use word identification skills such as sounding it out, looking for other word clues in the sentence, or breaking words into parts for unknown words

Using these strategies allows you to find a way to help identify an unknown word when you read that's difficult to pronounce.

N = Notice and check parts you don't understand and reread or read on

"Notice and check parts" entails placing a check mark in the margin next to the parts you don't understand in the text selection, deciding to reread that section again, or skipping it and going back to it after you're finished reading.

Note. From "SCAN and RUN: A Reading Comprehension Strategy That Works," by G. B. Salembier, 1999, *Journal of Adolescent and Adult Literacy.* Copyright ©1999 by *Journal of Adolescent and Adult Literacy.* Adapted with permission.

Academy of Orton-Gillingham Practitioners and Educators (2004). *What is the Orton-Gillingham approach?* Retrieved January 7, 2005, from http://www.ortonacademy .org/approach.html

Adler, B. (2001). *What is dyscalculia?* Retrieved July 31, 2005, from http://www.dyscalculiainfo.org

American-Speech-Language-Hearing Association. (2003). Code of ethics (Revised). *ASHA Supplement*, 23, 13–15.

Babbit, B. C. (1999). 10 tips for software selection for math instruction. *LD-Online Newsletter.* Retrieved August 5, 2005, from http://www.ldonline.org/ld_indepth/technology/babbitt_math_tips.html

Baum, S. (1990). *Gifted but learning disabled: A puzzling paradox.* (ERIC EC Digest #E479). Reston, VA: ERIC Clearinghouse on Disabilities and Gifted Education. (ERIC Document Reproduction Service No. ED321484).

Baum, S. M., Owen, S. V., & Dixon, J. (1991). *To be gifted and learning disabled: From identification to practical intervention strategies.* Mansfield Center, CT: Creative Learning Press.

Beckley, D. (1998). Gifted and learning disabled: Twice-exceptional students. *NRC/GT 1998 Spring Newsletter.*

Retrieved August 5, 2005, from http://www.gifted.uconn. edu/nrcgt/newsletter/spring98/sprng984.html

Bergert, S. (2000). *The warning signs of learning disabilities.* (ERIC EC Digest #E603). Reston, VA: ERIC Clearinghouse on Disabilities and Gifted Education. (ERIC Document Reproduction Service No. ED449633).

Brody, L. E. & Mills, J. C. (1997). Gifted children with learning disabilities: A review of the issues. *Journal of Learning Disabilities, 30,* 282–297.

Bull, L. (2003). The use of support group by parents of children with dyslexia. *Early Child Development and Care, 173,* 341–347.

Cicci, R. (1995). *What is wrong with me? Learning disabilities at home and school.* Timonium, MD: York Press.

Cline, S., & Schwartz, D. (1999). *Diverse populations of gifted children.* Upper Saddle River, NJ: Prentice Hall.

Cooper, E. E., Ness, M., & Smith, M. (2004). A case study of a child with dyslexia and spatial-temporal gifts. *Gifted Child Quarterly, 48,* 83–94.

Cooper, J. D. (2000). *Literacy: Helping children construct meaning* (4th ed.). New York: Houghton Mifflin Company.

deBettencourt, L. U. (2002). Understanding the differences between IDEA and Section 504. *Teaching Exceptional Children, 34*(3), 16–23.

Fetzer, E. A. (2000). The gifted/learning-disabled child: A guide for teachers and parents. *Gifted Child Today, 23(4),* 44–51.

EducationWorld.com (2003). *Weekly progress report.* Retrieved July 31, 2005, from http://www.education-world.com/ tools_templates/WeeklyProgressReport.doc

Geary, D. C. (1999). *Mathematical disabilities: What we know and don't know.* Retrieved July 25, 2005, from http://www.ldon line.org/ld_indepth/math_skills/geary_math_dis.html

Hannah, C. L., & Shore, B. M. (1995). Metacognition and high intellectual ability: Insights from the study of learning-disabled gifted students. *Gifted Child Quarterly, 39,* 95–110.

Hayes, P.A. (1993). *An examination of the spontaneously generated and retold narratives produced by gifted/learning disabled adolescents from an integrated perspective of language development.* Unpublished doctoral dissertation, Louisiana State University, Baton Rouge.

Hayes, P. A., & Norris, J. (1998). Evidence of language problems in underachieving gifted adolescents: Implications for assessment. *Journal of Secondary Gifted Education, 9*, 179–194.

Herold, J (2003). Teaching methods for dyslexic children. *Dyslexia Online Magazine.* Retrieved October 24, 2004, from http://www.dyslexia-parent.com/mag42.html

Hua, C. B., & Coleman, M. R. (2002). Preparing twice-exceptional children for adult lives: A critical need. *Understanding Our Gifted, 14*(2), 17–19.

Individuals with Disabilities Education Improvement Act of 2004, U.S.C. 118, § 2647 (2004).

International Dyslexia Association (2000). *Dyslexia basics.* Retrieved October 5, 2004, from http://www.interdys.org/pdf/basics.pdf

Jongsma, K. (1999/2000). Vocabulary and comprehension strategy development. *The Reading Teacher, 53*, 310–312.

Keller, E. (2004). *Dyscalculia.* Retrieved October 29, 2004, from http://www.as.wvu.edu/~scidis/dyscalcula.html

Learning Disabilities of America (1999). Nurturing oral language skills in infants and young children. Retrieved November 6, 2004, from http://www.ldonline.org/ld_in depth/speech-language/lda_oral_lang.html

Lidz, C. S. (2002). Mediated learning experience (MLE) as a basis for alternative approach to assessment. *School Psychology International, 23*, 68–84.

Little, C. (2001). A closer look at gifted children with disabilities. *Gifted Child Today, 24*, 46–52.

MATHCOUNTS Foundation (2004). *Problem solving strategies.* Retrieved November 9, 2004, from http://www.mathcounts.org/webarticles/articlefiles/155Problem%20Solving.pdf

Mather, D. S. (2003). Dyslexia and dysgraphia: More than written language difficulties in common. *Journal of Learning Disabilities, 36*, 307–317.

Mather, N., & Goldstein, S. (2001). Thinking with language,

images, and strategies. Retrieved July 25, 2005, from http://www.ldonline.org/ld_indepth/speech-language/thinking_with_language.html

McGuire, K. L., & Yewchuk, C. R. (1996). Use of metacognitive reading strategies by gifted/learning disabled students: An exploratory study. *Journal for the Education of the Gifted, 19*, 293–314.

Montague, M. (1991). Gifted and learning-disabled/gifted students' knowledge and use of mathematical problem-solving strategies. *Journal for the Education of the Gifted, 14*, 393–411.

National Association for Gifted Children (2004). *Legislative update. 108th Congress wrap-up.* Retrieved January 7, 2005, from http://www.nagc.org/Policy/update.html

Newman, R. M. (1998). *Gifted and math learning disabled: The dyscalculia syndrome.* Retrieved July 31, 2005, from http://www.dyscalculia.org/Edu561.html

Newman, R. M. (1997). *Memorizing facts: A multi-sensory solution.* Retrieved July 31, 2005, from http://www.dyscalculia.org/MemFacts.html

Olenchak, F. R., & Reis, S. M. (2002). Gifted students with learning disabilities. In M. Neihart, S. M. Reis, N. M. Robinson, & S. M. Moon (Eds.) *The social and emotional development of gifted children: What do we know?* (pp. 177–191). Waco, TX: Prufrock Press.

Rehabilitation Act of 1973, 29 U.S.C. § 701 et seq. (1973).

Richards, R. G. (1999). Strategies for dealing with dysgraphia. *LD-Online Newsletter.* Retrieved October 30, 2004, from http://www.ldonline.org/ld_indepth/writing/dysgraphia_strategies.html

Rock, M. L. (2005). Use of strategic self-monitoring to enhance academic engagement, productivity, and accuracy of students with and without exceptionalities. *Journal of Positive Behavior Interventions, 7*, 3–17.

Rosenfield, S. J. (n.d.). *Section 504 and IDEA: Basic similarities and differences.* Retrieved July 25, 2005, from http://www.ldonline.org/ld_indepth/legal_legislative/edlaw504.html

Salembier, G. B. (1999). SCAN and RUN: A reading comprehension strategy that works. *Journal of Adolescent & Adult Literacy, 42*, 386–394.

Shaywitz, S. E., & Shaywitz, B. A. (2004). Reading disability and the brain. *Educational Leadership, 61*(6), 6–11.

Siegle, L. M. (2004). *The complete guide: How to advocate for your special ed child* (3rd ed.). Berkeley, CA: Nolo.

Sevier County Department of Special Education (2004a). *Individuals with Disabilities Education Act.* Retrieved October 16, 2004, from http://www.slc.sevier.org/ idealong.htm

Sevier County Department of Special Education (2004b). *Section 504 made easy.* Retrieved October 16, 2004, from http://www.slc.sevier.org/504easy.doc

Sevier County Department of Special Education (2004c). *Tips for teachers on developing 504 accommodation plans.* Retrieved October 16, 2004, from http://www.slc.sevier.org/teacher-tipson504behaviorplans.doc

Smith, T. E. C. (2002). Section 504: What teachers need to know. *Intervention in School and Clinic, 37*, 259–266.

Stringer, S. J., Morton, R. C., & Bonikowski, M. H. (1999). Learning disabled students: Using process writing to build autonomy and self-esteem. *Journal of Instructional Psychology, 26*, 196–201.

Strop, J., & Goldman, D. (2002). The affective side: Emotional issues of twice-exceptional students. *Understanding Our Gifted, 14*(2), 28–29.

Swanson, H. L. (2001). Research on interventions for adolescents with learning disabilities: A meta-analysis of outcomes related to higher-order processing. *The Elementary School Journal, 101*, 331–348.

U.S. Department of Education Office of Intergovernmental and Interagency Affairs (2002). *Helping your child become a reader.* Washington, DC: Author.

Vaidya, S. R. (1993). Gifted children with learning disabilities: Theoretical implication and instructional challenge. *Education, 113*, 568–574.

Winebrenner, S. (2002). Strategies for teaching twice-exceptional students. *Understanding Our Gifted, 14*(2), 3–6.

Winebrenner, S. (2003). Teaching strategies for twice-exceptional students. *Intervention in School and Clinic, 38*, 131–137.

Yates, C. M. Berninger, V. W., & Abbott, R. D. (1995). Specific writing disabilities in intellectually gifted children. *Journal for the Education of the Gifted, 18*, 131–155.

Yell, M. L. (1998). *The law and special education*. Upper Saddle River, NJ: Prentice Hall.

Kevin Besnoy received his Ph.D. in curriculum, instruction, and special education with an emphasis in gifted education from The University of Southern Mississippi. During the 2003–2004 school year, he served as the project coordinator on a grant entitled "Appropriate Practices for Screening, Identifying, and Instructing Gifted/Disabled Youth." In addition to working at The Frances A. Karnes Center for Gifted Studies, he is an active member in the National Association for Gifted Children. His research interests include integrating technology into the gifted education curriculum and serving at-risk gifted youth.